Fred Bock

Piano Favorites for Quiet Reflection

CONTENTS

Fred Bock Music Company

I0808674

FOREWORD

May, 2002

Most people don't think of my father as being a quiet, reflective person. Chances are, you don't either. I don't blame you. My dad was a public figure who conducted, spoke and performed around the world. He loved sharing music and ideas with anyone who wanted to listen. Sometimes his efforts would leave a lasting impression on a listener. His words and music changed lives.

But most often, my dad is remembered for his stories and jokes. I know this is true because that is what everyone tells me. No matter where I go, people share with me their favorite Fred story. And most share more than one. Invariably, the memories lead to the retelling of one of his jokes or witty remarks that had left the room howling. Especially at the most inappropriate times.

My favorite recollection that someone shared with me happened shortly before he passed away. He and a couple of friends attended a showing of the movie, Saving Private Ryan. At the end of the opening, 30-minute scene, there is a long shot of the beach of Normandy in the aftermath of the D-Day invasion. Boats and bodies lie broken and abandoned on the sands. The surf is red with blood. Debris is everywhere, including hundreds of fish that had been killed by the exploding shells. In the utter stillness of the theater, Fred quietly commented with the wisdom of an old uncle: "Those fish were in the wrong place at the wrong time."

Now, it may seem insensitive and out of place telling this story, but I guarantee that the next time you see this scene with all those fish, you'll laugh out loud. I know this is true because it happened to me!

While funny Fred stories seem to abound like cornfields in Iowa, I have never had anyone tell me how "quiet and reflective" he or she found my father to be. The reason for this is because my dad never showed the quiet, reflective part of himself to many people. But, this side of his personality did exist. And more often than not, it appeared when he was sitting at the piano.

For Christ, a retreat into the wilderness brought Him closer to God. For me, I choose to walk in the quiet hallways of a museum. For my dad, the piano was the balm that soothed the frayed nerves and calmed his spirit. I know this is true because I saw it. He would start to play, close his eyes, and be transported to another place. I believe that God spoke to him directly through the notes that came from that piano. And the message was "Be still and know that I am God."

At the end of the day, isn't that what we all need to hear? Don't we want to be reminded that despite all the stresses and worries and uncertainty in our lives, God is still God and that He's in control of it all? So, when the world seems like it's closing in and there's no help in sight, I urge you to go to a piano and play one of these arrangements. Let your heart hear the Spirit speaking to you through the notes. God will soothe your nerves and calm your spirit like He did for my father so many times. I know this is true because He's done it for me.

Best Wishes.

Stephen Bock
Tarzana, California

Be Still and Know

Traditional Melody
Arranged by Fred Bock

f
mp
mf
simile
f
f

a little stronger and broader
ten.
ten.
f
sub. p
mf
ten.
ten.
mp
mf
mf
mp
p
pp

Come Share the Lord

Bryan Jeffery Leech
Arranged by Fred Bock

a tempo

brighter
mf
(echo)
mf

ten.
ten.
ten.
ten.
a little brighter
ten.
ten.
ten.
slowing
ten.
ten.
a tempo
no ritard.

Give Thanks

Henry Smith
Arranged by Fred Bock

f
ff
l.h.

ff
mf
mp
mf
a little faster
ff

ten.
gradually slowing
ff
f
mf
mp
mp
slight accel.
rit.
pp

He Is Lord

Traditional
Arranged by Fred Bock

Moderato (♩=72)

rit.
Strongly
f
mf
f
mp
ten.
ten.
ten.
mf
f
ten.
ten.
r.h.
l.h.
subito
p
mf
mf
f

Healer of Broken Hearts

Georgia Stiffler
Arranged by Fred Bock

Freely, not rhythmically

2nd time
Fine
ad lib., freely
mf
Ped
D. S. al Fine
8ba

Just As I Am

William B. Bradbury
Arranged by Fred Bock

Tenderly (♩ =80)

a little faster
slowing

5
2
1
a tempo
(♭)
l.h.
mf
r.h.
mp
p
8ba

On Eagle's Wings

Michael Joncas
Arranged by Fred Bock

With affirmation (♩ =84)

ten.
f
ten.
mp
mf
mf
f
a little brighter
1

p
mf
f
mf
f
mp
mf
rit.
r.h.

Precious Lord, Take My Hand

Traditional Spiritual
Arranged by Fred Bock

roll
down
8va
f
8va
2
(♭)

8va
loco
8va
f
8va
2
2
2
8va
p

The Hiding Place

Bryan Jeffery Leech
Arranged by Fred Bock

Easily, but with assurance

a little faster
ten.
ten.
f
mf

ten.
ten.
ten.
ten.
ten.
8va

What a Friend We Have in Jesus

Charles Converse
Arranged by Fred Bock

* *Downstem notes should be held down to sustain.*

a little faster

f
f
mf
L.H.
R.H.
Very gently
mp
p
(slow roll up)
ten.
mf
ten.
mp
8va
pp
8va